TERRACES AND BALCONIES

TERRASSES ET BALCONS

TERRASSEN UND BALKONE

TERRACES AND BALCONIES
TERRASSES ET BALCONS
TERRASSEN UND BALKONE

evergreen

© 2008 EVERGREEN GmbH

Editorial coordination, editor:
Simone Schleifer

Texts:
Florian Seidel

English translation:
Hazel Britton for LocTeam, Barcelona

French translation:
Claire Débard for LocTeam, Barcelona

German proof-reading:
André Höchemer for LocTeam, Barcelona

Typesetting and text editing:
LocTeam, Barcelona

Art director:
Mireia Casanovas Soley

Graphic design and layout:
Laura Millán

Printed in Spain

ISBN 978-3-8365-0395-2

Contents Sommaire Inhalt

 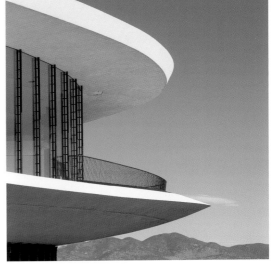

Terraces and balconies have always been an essential architectural feature – they are effectively the continuation of a dwelling outdoors. From the point of view of architectural history, however, there were a host of reasons behind the development of terraces and balconies.

With the terrace, both landscape and house take on a kind of symbolic connection, which is already suggested in the word's Latin root, terra, meaning "earth" or "land".

All over the world, a good portion of domestic life has always been played out on the terrace, wherever the climate allows. Only at night or in inclement weather did our forefathers withdraw into their dark houses with their few, narrow window openings. The terrace underwent an important development in the Baroque period with the construction of the castles and country houses. The so-called *parterre* formed the transition from the park, in French or English style, to the architecture of the castle.

Modern architecture has unified both lines of development and created an extremely versatile integration of an indoor and outdoor space, and as a result, the terrace often becomes the hub of a house. Le Corbusier even declared the terrace, in the form of a roof garden, to be one of the five definitive elements of a new architecture, so essential did he view this continuation and crowning of the modern house under the open sky.

The balcony, on the other hand, is a much newer construction feature than the terrace. The word comes from the German Balken, meaning "beam", and suggests that the balcony required added structural work, which entailed the corresponding financial means.

Thus, the balcony at first only appeared in buildings erected by the gentry and clergy, above all in urban architecture. Since time immemorial, the ruler of the people has presented him- or herself on the balcony, and from the balcony holy relics were shown to believers. The balcony and loggia were originally reserved for urban areas and play an important role in this setting.

Not until the modern age did the balcony lose its function as a place of presentation and come to be interpreted in a completely new way. It has become an individual leisure space, a garden substitute, as land and soil are not available in the crowded city. Nowadays, in many countries balconies are one of the home's basic features. Here, city dwellers can relax after their workday and enjoy their private pleasures. The balcony becomes an oasis, a secret paradise, and its original meaning has become increasingly lost in time.

The ever-growing importance of leisure gives the individually-created balcony increasing significance, and size as well as design accordingly take on extra meaning. With their organic lines, balconies bring new forms to the façades of residential buildings, so becoming representative elements.

This book introduces terraces and balconies from all over the world that have been created by well-known architects and designers and that are particularly original or successfully unite aesthetics and functionality.

Terrasses et balcons font depuis toujours partie intégrante de l'architecture. Ils constituent pour ainsi dire un prolongement extérieur du logis. Du point de vue de l'histoire de la construction cependant, les raisons qui ont mené à l'émergence des terrasses et des balcons sont très différentes.

La terrasse crée entre le paysage et l'habitation une sorte de lien symbolique, déjà suggéré par la racine latine du mot, *terra*, terre ou pays.

Partout où le climat l'a permis, depuis la construction des premières habitations, une grande partie de la vie domestique s'est déroulée sur la terrasse. On ne se retirait que pour la nuit ou par mauvais temps à l'intérieur de la maison, qui ne possédait généralement que quelques ouvertures étroites en guise de fenêtres, à condition encore d'en avoir possédé, et restait donc plutôt sombre. L'architecture des châteaux et manoirs baroques a été déterminante pour le développement des terrasses : le jardin appelé parterre faisait désormais la transition entre le parc à l'anglaise ou le jardin à la française et le château.

L'architecture de l'époque moderne a fusionné les deux courants de l'évolution et pour faire s'interpénétrer, sous des formes extrêmement variées, les espaces intérieur et extérieur, la terrasse devenant souvent le centre de la maison. Le Corbusier va jusqu'à considérer le toit-jardin comme l'un des cinq éléments fondamentaux d'une architecture nouvelle, tant ce prolongement et ce couronnement à ciel ouvert des habitations modernes lui semblent essentiels.

Le balcon, quant à lui, est un élément de construction beaucoup plus récent que la terrasse. Le mot vient de l'allemand *Balken*, qui signifie « poutre » ou « pilier » et laisse entrevoir qu'un balcon nécessitait un investissement de construction plus important, ce qui supposait les moyens financiers appropriés.

C'est la raison pour laquelle le balcon est d'abord apparu sur les bâtiments de la noblesse et du clergé, et donc surtout dans les villes. De tout temps, le souverain s'est présenté à son peuple depuis le balcon et de saintes reliques y ont été exhibées aux croyants. Balcon et loggia sont depuis l'origine réservés à l'espace urbain et y jouent un rôle important.

Il faudra attendre l'époque moderne pour voir le balcon perdre sa fonction représentative et être totalement réinterprété. Il devient alors un espace de liberté individuelle, un jardin de substitution partout où l'étroitesse des villes rend le terrain inaccessible. Dans de nombreux pays, le balcon fait désormais partie des éléments de base d'un logement. On peut s'y détendre après le travail quotidien et y savourer son bonheur intime ; le balcon devient une oasis, un paradis chez soi et sa fonction originelle tombe peu à peu dans l'oubli.

La place croissante qu'occupe le temps libre dans l'existence explique l'importance, elle aussi toujours plus grande, accordée au balcon aménagé individuellement, d'où la valeur accrue prise également par sa taille et sa conception. Les structures des balcons en saillie redécoupent les façades des immeubles, leur donnent des formes nouvelles et en deviennent des éléments particulièrement représentatifs.

Cet ouvrage présente des terrasses et des balcons créés dans le monde entier par des architectes et des designers de renom, qui se distinguent par leur grande originalité ou concilient avec succès esthétique et fonctionnalité.

Terrassen und Balkone bilden seit jeher feste Bestandteile der Architektur – sie sind gewissermaßen die Fortsetzung der menschlichen Behausung unter freiem Himmel. Unter baugeschichtllichen Gesichtspunkten führten allerdings sehr unterschiedliche Gründe zur Entstehung von Terrassen und Balkonen.

Landschaft und Haus gehen bei der Terrasse eine Art symbolischer Verbindung ein, die das schon im Begriff enthaltene lateinische Wort *terra*, Erde oder Land, nahe legt.

Überall auf der Welt, wo es das Klima erlaubte, spielte sich seit der Errichtung der ersten Behausungen ein Großteil des häuslichen Lebens weitgehend auf der Terrasse ab. Lediglich bei Nacht oder schlechtem Wetter zog man sich ins Haus zurück, das, wenn überhaupt, zumeist nur wenige, schmale Fensteröffnungen besaß und damit dunkel war. In der Architektur von Schlössern und Landhäusern des Barock wurde die Terrasse entscheidend weiter entwickelt. Das so genannte Gartenparterre bildete den Übergang des im französischen oder englischen Stil gestalteten Parks zur Architektur des Schlosses.

Die Architektur der Moderne hat die beiden Entwicklungslinien vereint und eine äußerst vielfältige Verflechtung von Innen- und Außenraum geschaffen, wobei die Terrasse häufig zum Dreh- und Angelpunkt eines Hauses wird. Le Corbusier erklärt die Terrasse, in Form des Dachgartens, sogar zu einem der fünf maßgeblichen Elemente einer neuen Architektur, so essentiell scheint ihm diese Fortsetzung und Bekrönung des modernen Hauses unter freiem Himmel gewesen zu sein.

Der Balkon hingegen ist als Bauelement viel jünger als die Terrasse. Die Bezeichnung stammt vom deutschen Balken ab. Sie lässt erahnen, dass der Balkon einen erhöhten konstruktiven Aufwand erforderte, der die entsprechenden finanziellen Mittel voraussetzte.

Der Balkon trat daher zunächst nur in den von Adel und Klerus errichteten Gebäuden in Erscheinung, vor allem also in der städtischen Architektur. Vom Balkon aus präsentierte sich seit alters her der Herrscher dem Volk oder heilige Reliquien wurden von dort den Gläubigen gezeigt. Der Balkon und die Loggia sind von ihrem Ursprung her dem städtischen Raum vorbehalten und spielen darin eine wichtige Rolle.

Erst in der Moderne verliert der Balkon seine Funktion als Ort der Repräsentation und wird vollkommen neu interpretiert. Er wird zum individuellen Freiraum, zum Gartenersatz, wenn eigener Grund und Boden in der Enge der Städte nicht verfügbar sind. Ein eigener Balkon gehört mittlerweile in vielen Ländern zum Grundbestandteil einer Wohnung. Hier kann sich der Bewohner von der täglichen Arbeit entspannen und sein privates Glück genießen. Der Balkon wird zur Oase, zum heimischen Paradies, und sein ursprünglicher Sinn gerät zunehmend in Vergessenheit.

Der ständig steigende Stellenwert der Freizeit im Leben der Menschen lässt den individuell gestalteten Balkon heute immer wichtiger werden, und Größe sowie Ausführung eines Balkons gewinnen dadurch an Bedeutung. Plastisch geformte Balkone gliedern in neuen Formen die Fassaden von Wohngebäuden und werden solcherart zu repräsentativen Elementen.

Dieses Buch stellt Terrassen und Balkone aus aller Welt vor, die von bekannten Architekten und Designern geschaffen wurden und besonders originell sind oder gelungen Ästhetik und Funktionalität vereinen.

Terraces

Terrasses

Terrassen

Terraces are mostly directly related to the landscape surrounding a building. They can frame a view — for instance, through canopies or side walls — they can imitate particular landscape elements on their own more human scale, or they can enable the landscape to be perceived and experienced in a different way. Often one first becomes aware of the landscape through the design of the terrace, perhaps through trees offering shade, a cooling pool, or a shield against the wind. Expertly created terraces reflect elements of their surrounding landscapes, such as stone, wood, plants or water. The spirit and atmosphere of the surroundings are reduced to their essence, the world recreated in microcosm. The landscape becomes a part of the house and the life of the house.

Les terrasses ont généralement un lien direct avec le paysage qui entoure un bâtiment. Elles peuvent encadrer une vue, notamment au moyen d'auvents ou de parois latérales, elles peuvent reprendre certains éléments du paysage à l'échelle de la terrasse, et donc à échelle humaine, ou favoriser une autre perception de la nature. C'est souvent ultérieurement à sa réalisation qu'une terrasse fait prendre conscience d'un décor naturel grâce, par exemple, à des arbres qui dispensent de l'ombre, à un bassin qui rafraîchit ou à une protection contre le vent. Les terrasses les plus réussies comprennent des éléments de leur environnement proche tels que des pierres, du bois, des plantations ou de l'eau. L'âme et l'atmosphère d'un lieu y sont concentrées jusqu'à devenir l'essence même de ces terrasses, le monde y est recréé en microcosme. Le paysage est intégré à la maison et à la vie.

Terrassen haben zumeist einen direkten Bezug auf die Landschaft, die ein Gebäude umgibt. Sie können einen Blick rahmen, etwa durch Vordächer oder Seitenwände, sie können bestimmte landschaftliche Elemente im Maßstab der Terrasse und damit des Menschen nachempfinden oder die Landschaft auf andere Weise spürbar und erlebbar machen. Oft wird erst durch die Ausführung der Terrasse die Landschaft erfahrbar, etwa durch schattenspendende Bäume, ein kühlendes Wasserbecken oder eine Abschirmung gegen den Wind. Meisterhaft gestaltete Terrassen spiegeln Elemente der jeweiligen Landschaft wider, wie etwa Stein, Holz, Bepflanzung oder Wasser. Der Geist und die Atmosphäre der Umgebung werden zur Essenz verdichtet, die Welt als Mikrokosmos nachgebildet. Die Landschaft wird zum Teil des Hauses und des Lebens im Haus.

14-17: The characteristic elements of this terrace are wood, concrete and water. They blend in harmoniously with the natural surroundings, yet stand in clear contrast to the rough, craggy coastal landscape. In this way, the terrace mediates between nature and the house.

14-17 : La terrasse est caractérisée par les éléments bois, béton et eau. Ils s'intègrent harmonieusement dans le paysage naturel mais forment néanmoins un contraste net avec la côte sauvage et découpée. La terrasse fait transition entre la nature et l'habitation.

14-17: Die charakteristischen Elemente dieser Terrasse sind Holz, Beton und Wasser. Sie fügen sich harmonisch in die natürliche Umgebung ein, bilden jedoch einen deutlichen Kontrast zur rauen, zerklüfteten Küstenlandschaft. Die Terrasse vermittelt auf diese Weise zwischen Natur und Haus.

2-25: The plants that seem to well up from under the wooden deck embody the city dweller's dream: the metamorphosis of the city landscape into an idyll of nature.

2-25 : Les plantes, qui semblent percer le revêtement en bois, incarnent le rêve de tout citadin : la métamorphose du paysage urbain en une idylle naturelle.

2-25: Die Pflanzen, die unter dem Holzdeck hervorzubrechen scheinen, verkörpern den Traum des Städters: die Metamorphose der Stadtlandschaft in eine Naturidylle.

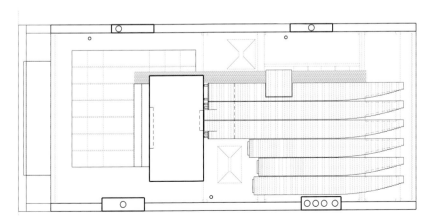

Roof plan Plan du toit Dachgeschoss

30-33: This terrace is characterised by clear horizontal lines. Wide sliding doors make for a smooth transition from indoors to outdoors. The projecting first storey provides additional shade.

30-33 : La terrasse est caractérisée par des lignes horizontales claires. De larges portes coulissantes permettent un passage fluide de l'intérieur vers l'extérieur. Le volume saillant dispense une ombre supplémentaire.

30-33: Die Terrasse ist von klaren, horizontalen Linien geprägt. Breite Schiebetüren ermöglichen einen fließenden Übergang von innen nach außen. Das auskragende Volumen sorgt für zusätzlichen Schatten.

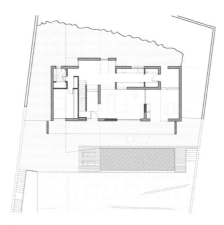

Plan Plan Grundriss

34-37: The flagstone terrace is accessible from the living room through large sliding doors and thus opens the interior to the outdoors. The louvered blinds, in contrast, allow for withdrawal and privacy when needed.

34-37 : La terrasse carrelée est accessible depuis la salle de séjour par de grandes portes coulissantes qui ouvrent l'intérieur vers l'extérieur, tandis que des volets accordéon coulissants permettent un verrouillage hermétique.

34-37: Diese mit Fliesen belegte Terrasse ist durch große Schiebetüren vom Wohnraum her begehbar und öffnet so den Innenraum nach außen. Faltschiebeläden dagegen erlauben eine hermetische Abriegelung.

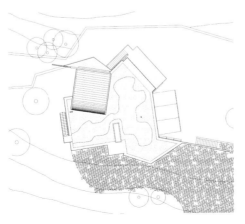

Site plan Plan de situation Umgebungsplan

8-39: High above the sea, this wooden terrace offers wonderful views. The balustrade, made of sturdy black steel with all-around glass panels, safeguards the terrace and protects it from wind. The gnarled old tree offers shade and stands in contrast to the modern, angular form of the house.

8-39 : Cette terrasse en bois, qui surplombe la mer de très haut, offre une vue magnifique. La balustrade contournante, constituée de solides profilés d'acier noirs et d'éléments vitrés, protège la terrasse contre le vent et garantit sa sécurité. Le vieil arbre noueux dispense de l'ombre et contraste avec les formes modernes et anguleuses de la maison.

8-39: Hoch über dem Meer bietet diese Terrasse aus Holz einen wundervollen Ausblick. Das aus starken, schwarzen Stahlprofilen gefertigte Geländer mit rund umlaufenden Glaselementen schützt vor dem Wind und sichert die Terrasse. Der knorrige alte Baum spendet Schatten und steht im Kontrast zu den modernen, kantigen Formen des Hauses.

40-41: This wooden terrace is separated from the hard, contrasting materials of the swimming pool and the parapet by a narrow strip of spotless white gravel and pebbles. Through the transparent walls, the terrace seems to become one with the horizon.

40-41 : La terrasse en bois est séparée des matériaux durs et contrastants de la piscine et de la balustrade par une bande étroite de gravier d'un blanc éclatant. Grâc à la transparence de la balustrade, la terrasse semble se fondre avec l'horizon.

40-41: Die Holz-Terrasse ist von den harten, kontrastierenden Materialien des Schwimmbeckens und der Brüstung durch einen schmalen Streifen mit strahlend weißem Kies abgesetzt. Durch die Transparenz der Brüstung scheint die Terrasse eins zu werden mit dem Horizont.

2-43: Enclosed by white mud walls with a few relatively small window openings, this terrace seems like an altogether cosy room under the open sky. This impression is ~inforced by the garden furniture.

2-43 : Encadrée par des murs blanchis à la chaux et aux ouvertures relativement petites, la terrasse fait penser à une chambre à ciel ouvert très confortable, une ~npression encore renforcée par le choix du mobilier.

2-43: Von weiß geschlämmten Wänden mit relativ kleinen Fensteröffnungen eingefasst, wirkt die Terrasse wie ein urgemütliches Zimmer unter freiem Himmel. Durch ~e Möblierung wird dieser Eindruck noch verstärkt.

4-47: Glass, wood and concrete form two contrasting, masterfully-proportioned outdoor rooms in the minimalist style. A generously-sized court with swimming pool complemented by a small, intimate patio.

4-47 : Verre, bois et béton délimitent deux pièces extérieures opposées, aménagées dans un style minimaliste et parfaitement proportionnées : une cour spacieuse avec piscine et un petit patio plus intime.

4-47: Glas, Holz und Beton formen zwei gegensätzliche, minimalistisch gestaltete und meisterhaft proportionierte Außenräume: einen großzügigen Hof mit Schwimmbecken und einen kleinen, intimen Patio.

3-51: Powerful columns supporting the canopy roof and a grid-like arrangement of palms lend character to this terrace, which overlooks a swimming pool.

3-51 : La terrasse, face à la piscine, est divisée par les épais piliers, qui portent l'auvent, et les palmiers plantés en damiers.

3-51: Mächtige Stützen, die das Vordach tragen, und im Raster gepflanzte Palmen gliedern diese Terrasse, der ein Swimmingpool vorgelagert ist.

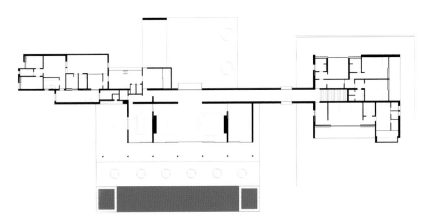

Ground floor Rez-de-chaussée Erdgeschoss

4-55: The natural incline was cleverly used to structure this terrace. On the lowest tier, there is a long, cushioned stone bench, and in front there are two small dipping pools where visitors can cool off. The colours and materials of the house and the terrace combine with the vegetation and water to form a harmonious whole— an invitation to relax.

4-55 : La déclivité naturelle est habilement exploitée pour diviser la terrasse en plusieurs espaces. Au niveau inférieur, deux petits bassins face à un banc de pierre contribuent à rafraîchir le tout. Les couleurs et les matières de la maison et de la terrasse s'associent à la végétation et à l'eau pour former un ensemble harmonieux qui invite à la détente.

4-55: Das natürliche Gefälle wird geschickt ausgenutzt, um die Terrasse zu gliedern. Auf der untersten Stufe befindet sich eine steinerne Sitzbank, davor liegen zwei kleine Wasserbecken, die der Abkühlung dienen. Die Farben und Materialien des Hauses und der Terrasse verbinden sich mit der Vegetation und dem Wasser zu einer harmonischen Einheit, die zum Entspannen einlädt.

56-59: A wall of natural rock, the backdrop for a curtain of flowing water, contrasts with the clearly-structured house. In the narrow area between both, there is enough space for a shady oasis.

56-59 : Le mur de pierre naturelle et l'eau courante contrastent avec la maison, aux structures claires et nettes. L'espace étroit les séparant suffit à abriter une oasis ombragée.

56-59: Eine Wand aus natürlichem Gestein, über das Wasser läuft, bildet einen Kontrast zum klar strukturierten Haus. Im schmalen Bereich dazwischen ist ausreichend Platz für eine schattige Oase.

62-65: The designers of this patio did not succumb to the temptation to produce an illusion of nature. Rather, they created a room drenched in light, impressive in its clarity and serenity.

62-65 : Les créateurs de ce patio n'ont pas cédé à la tentation de donner une illusion trompeuse de nature. Ils ont préféré concevoir un espace de lumière d'une impressionnante clarté.

62-65: Die Gestalter dieses Patios sind nicht der Versuchung erlegen, eine falsche Illusion von Natur zu erzeugen. Stattdessen haben sie einen Lichtraum von beeindruckender Klarheit geschaffen.

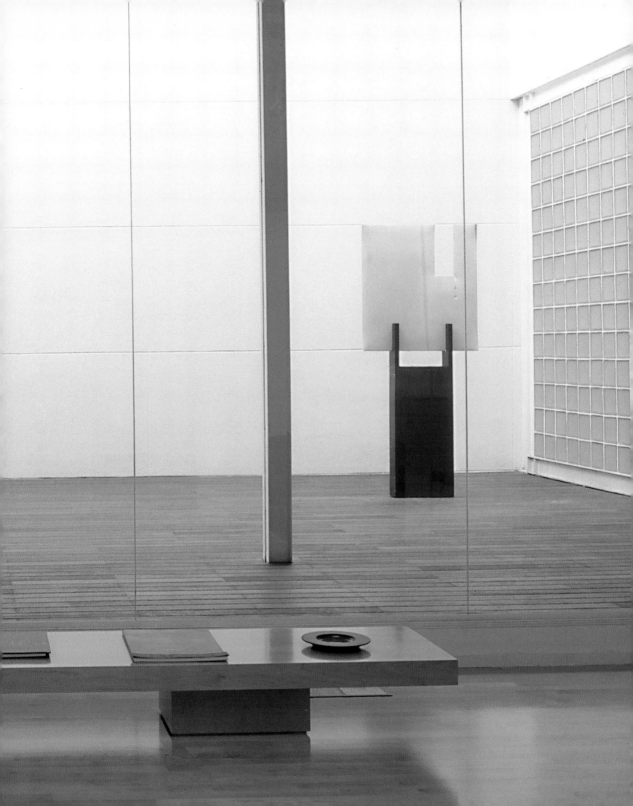

68-71: This terrace is arranged in three parts: a shady, covered haven; an open, green expanse; and an area of pure, white stone with a swimming pool at a right angl to this, stretching out towards the sea. Due to the high position, visitors can glimpse the sea between the trunks and tops of the trees.

68-71 : La terrasse est divisée en trois : une partie couverte et ombragée, un espace ouvert et une surface à angle droit avec piscine étirée vers de la mer. La surélévation donne vue sur la mer en contrebas à travers les troncs et les cimes d'arbres.

68-71: Die Terrasse gliedert sich in drei Teile: einen schattigen und überdeckten Bereich, ein offenes Areal und eine quer dazu liegende auf das Meer weisende Fläche mit einem Swimmingpool. Aufgrund der erhöhten Lage blickt man zwischen den Stämmen und Baumkronen hinunter aufs Meer.

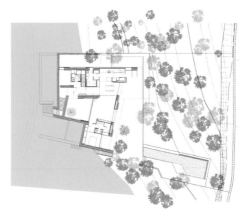

Plan Plan Grundriss

72-73: A light steel roof and a wooden deck: a terrace has been created with comparatively little effort or investment. It is generously proportioned, shaded from the sun and open on three sides.

72-73 : Toit métallique léger et plancher en bois : on obtient à relativement peu de frais une terrasse spacieuse, protégée du soleil et ouverte sur trois côtés.

72-73: Ein leichtes Stahldach und ein Holzdeck – mit vergleichsweise geringem Aufwand ist eine großzügig bemessene, sonnengeschützte und nach drei Seiten hin offene Terrasse entstanden.

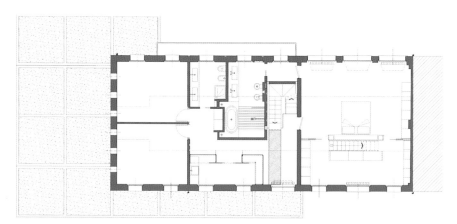

Ground floor Rez-de-chaussée Erdgeschoss

-77: The outdoor area of the house is characterised by a row of different terraces on various levels, each of which is individually designed. Some are open on all sides t the back and are reminiscent of a theatre stage. Others are effective with their high walls, irregular slate slabs and sturdy, shady trees.

-77 : L'extérieur de la maison est marqué par une série de terrasses aménagées à différents niveaux et conçues chacune de manière individuelle. Certaines sont vertes de toutes parts, sauf au fond, et ressemblent à la scène d'un théâtre. D'autres rappellent des oasis entourées de hauts murs aux ardoises irrégulières, ombragées r de grands arbres.

-77: Der Außenbereich des Hauses ist durch eine Reihe unterschiedlicher Terrassen geprägt, die auf verschiedenen Niveaus liegen und individuell gestaltet sind. Einige nd bis auf die Rückwand nach allen Seiten offen und erinnern an Theaterbühnen. Andere wirken durch hohe Mauern, unregelmäßig verlegten Schiefer und mächtige, hattenspendende Bäume wie Oasen.

2-83: This large terrace, extending over two levels, is situated high above the roofs of the town. The horizontal lines and the use of wood conjure up the image of a ship's deck.

2-83 : La grande terrasse à deux étages surplombe les toits de la ville. Ses lignes horizontales et le bois utilisé évoquent le pont d'un bateau.

2-83: Hoch über den Dächern der Stadt befindet sich die großzügige, über zwei Geschosse reichende Terrasse. Die horizontalen Linien und die Verwendung von Holz lassen die Assoziation an ein Schiffsdeck aufkommen.

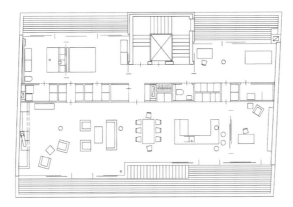

First floor Premier étage Erstes Obergeschoss

84-85: Simple, high-quality materials, like wood and natural stone, combined with gravel, water and a judicious use of plants, all give rise to an area with the meditative feel of a Zen garden.

84-85 : Des matières simples et nobles telles que le bois ou la pierre naturelle, associées à des graviers, ainsi que l'eau et les plantations appropriées créent l'atmosphère de méditation d'un jardin zen.

84-85: Einfache, edle Materialien, wie Holz oder Naturstein, kombiniert mit Kies, Wasser und entsprechender Bepflanzung lassen einen Bereich mit der meditativen Anmutung eines Zen-Gartens entstehen.

86-89: The living room can be completely opened to the terrace, so that the inner room and outer spaces can merge, in a manner of speaking; the choice of the same flooring material for the interior and the terrace underscores this intention. The terrace has a minimalist design; only a simple, concrete cantilevered sunroof and the flooring motifs bring structure to the large space. Nothing distracts from the wonderful view.

86-89 : Le salon peut s'ouvrir entièrement sur la terrasse, fusionnant pour ainsi dire les espaces intérieur et extérieur, une impression encore renforcée par le choix d'un matériau de sol identique dedans et dehors. L'aménagement de la terrasse est minimaliste. Seuls l'avant-toit en béton et les motifs de revêtement du sol coupent le vaste espace. Rien ne détourne le regard de la vue exceptionnelle.

86-89: Der Wohnraum lässt sich vollständig zur Terrasse hin öffnen, sodass Innen- und Außenraum gewissermaßen miteinander verschmelzen können; die Wahl des gleichen Fußbodenmaterials innen wie außen unterstreicht diese Intention. Die Terrasse ist minimalistisch gestaltet, nur ein einfaches, auskragendes Sonnendach aus Beton und die unterschiedlichen Felder des Bodenbelags gliedern den weiten Raum. Nichts lenkt von dem wunderbaren Ausblick ab.

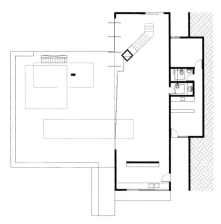

Plan Plan Grundriss

91: This terrace displays several subtle changes in height and features a varied combination of materials. The concrete, wood or water areas intertwine in an L-shape, enabling ever-changing constellations and relationships. Plants play a minor role in this highly aesthetic, formal composition.

91 : La terrasse à plusieurs niveaux différents est caracterisée par des combinaisons de matériaux très variés. Le béton, le bois et l'eau créent des espaces en L qui s'emboîtent les uns dans les autres, formant des constellations et des associations sans cesse nouvelles. La plantation est tributaire de la conception très esthétique, aux formes toutefois réduites.

91: Diese Terrasse zeigt verschiedene Höhenstaffelungen und wird durch abwechslungsreiche Kombinationen von Materialien geprägt. Die aus Beton, Holz oder Wasser gebildeten Bereiche greifen im Grundriss L-förmig ineinander und ermöglichen so immer neue Konstellationen und Bezüge. Die Bepflanzung wird der sehr ästhetischen, formal reduzierten Gestaltung untergeordnet.

92-95: An interesting and varied structure has been achieved in a comparatively small space. The blue of the water, the pink of the wall and the green of the surroundings dominate the totally harmonious colour concept of all the elements.

92-95 : L'espace a été structuré de manière intéressante et variée sur une surface relativement réduite. Le bleu de l'eau, le rose du mur et le vert de la nature dominent l'ensemble composé de plusieurs éléments aux couleurs harmonieusement assorties.

92-95: Auf vergleichsweise wenig Grundfläche ist hier ein interessantes und abwechslungsreiches Raumgefüge realisiert worden. Das Blau des Wassers, das Rosa der Wand und das Grün der Umgebung dominieren das insgesamt harmonisch aufeinander abgestimmte Farbkonzept aller Elemente.

99-103: A wide, whitewashed concrete sunroof is the only structural element in this wooden terrace. A low bench bordering the terrace also serves as a railing.

99-103 : Le long auvent en béton badigeonné de blanc constitue l'unique coupure de la terrasse en bois. Le banc en bois qui en fait le tour tient lieu de balustrade.

99-103: Ein weit gespanntes, weiß getünchtes Sonnendach aus Beton ist die einzige Gliederung der mit Holz gedeckten Terrasse. Eine niedrige, umlaufende Sitzbank aus Holz dient zugleich auch als Geländer.

Balconies

Balcons

Balkone

Balconies can become a house's calling card. Unlike terraces, balconies are first and foremost a structural element of a house epitomising the character of the building and its architectural style. The balcony can be the crowning glory of a house – the extension of the living room outdoors. It is, moreover, an important means of lending formality to a house and structuring a façade. The emphasis can be placed either on the individual, the extraordinary and the distinctive or on the powerful effect of repetition. The designer's art consists of finding a solution that both suits the inner logic and function of a house and is aesthetically pleasing.

Les balcons peuvent se révéler être les cartes de visite d'une maison. Contrairement à la terrasse, le balcon est avant tout une pièce rapportée, un élément qui incarne la nature du bâtiment et sa construction. Avec un balcon en prolongement extérieur du salon, une maison trouve son couronnement et son point final. Par ailleurs, il constitue le moyen idéal de diviser une habitation de manière formelle et de structurer une façade. L'accent peut alors être mis sur le caractère individuel, particulier et unique ou sur l'effet et la force de la répétition. Tout l'art du concepteur consiste à trouver une solution qui respecte la logique interne et la fonctionnalité d'une maison autant que l'esthétique.

Balkone können zur Visitenkarte eines Hauses werden. Anders als die Terrasse ist der Balkon zuallererst Bauteil, konstruktives Element eines Hauses, in dem sich das Wesen des Gebäudes und seine Bauweise verkörpern. Im Balkon als Fortführung des Wohnraums nach außen kann das Haus seine Bekrönung und seinen Abschluss finden. Der Balkon ist darüber hinaus ein wesentliches Mittel, ein Haus formal zu gliedern und eine Fassade zu strukturieren. Die Betonung kann dabei entweder auf die Individualität, das Besondere und Unverwechselbare gelegt werden oder die kraftvolle Wirkung der Repetition. Die Kunst des Gestalters besteht darin, eine Lösung zu finden, die sowohl der inneren Logik und Funktion eines Hauses als auch der Ästhetik gerecht wird.

06-107: On this apartment building, each balcony displays a coloured underside and side wall. In addition, they are placed on the left or right of the façade depending on the storey. The varied colours of the balconies form a diagonal pattern, which from a distance has a structured, orderly effect but up close underscores the individuality of each balcony.

06-107 : Les balcons de cet immeuble sont peints en couleur par dessous et sur un côté. Ils sont également décalés d'un étage sur l'autre, de sorte que les couleurs forment un motif en diagonale qui apparaît structuré et ordonné de loin mais souligne l'individualité de chaque balcon de près.

06-107: Bei diesem Apartmentblock sind die Balkonunterseiten und jeweils eine Seitenwand farbig gestaltet. Zusätzlich sind die Balkone jeweils geschossweise gegeneinander versetzt. Die unterschiedlichen Farben der Balkone bilden ein diagonales Muster, das aus der Entfernung strukturiert und geordnet wirkt, aus der Nähe jedoch die Individualität jedes einzelnen Balkons unterstreicht.

108-111: These balconies, which have been reduced to the simplest of forms, boast transparent panes in the most varied colour tones, filtering the view of the outdoors as well as the curious glances inside of passers-by.

108-111 : Réduits au strict minimum, les balcons sont dotés de plaques transparentes aux couleurs les plus variées pour filtrer la vue de l'intérieur vers l'extérieur ainsi que les regards curieux en sens inverse.

108-111: Die Balkone, auf das notwendige Minimum reduziert, verfügen über transparente Scheiben in den unterschiedlichsten Farbtönen, die sowohl den Ausblick von innen nach außen als auch den neugierigen Einblick ins Innere filtern.

112-114: With its red-painted wooden panels, this house stands in total contrast to the surrounding forest and wintry landscape. The loggia is completely integrated into the main part of the house, while the roof protects against heavy winter snowfall.

112-114 : Avec ses panneaux de bois peints en rouge, la maison forme un contraste parfait avec la forêt environnante et le paysage hivernal. La loggia est entièrement intégrée au volume d'habitation. Le toit la protège des fortes chutes de neige.

112-114: Das Haus steht durch seine rot gestrichenen Holzpaneele in vollkommenem Kontrast zur umgebenden Wald- und Winterlandschaft. Die Loggia ist vollständig in das Volumen des Hauses integriert. Das Dach schützt vor starkem Schneefall im Winter.

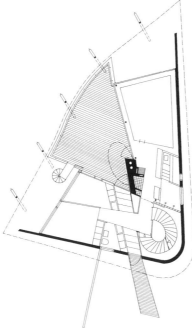

Plan Plan Grundriss

118-119: The spacious balcony, with its wooden panelling and partial camouflage thanks to a slanting screen, offers a uncluttered view of the landscape.

118-119 : Partiellement protégé des regards par un paravent incliné, le spacieux balcon en bois offre une vue directe sur le paysage environnant.

118-119: Der großzügig bemessene Balkon mit Holzbeplankung und teilweisem Sichtschutz durch einen schräg geneigten Schirm bietet einen unverstellten Ausblick die Landschaft.

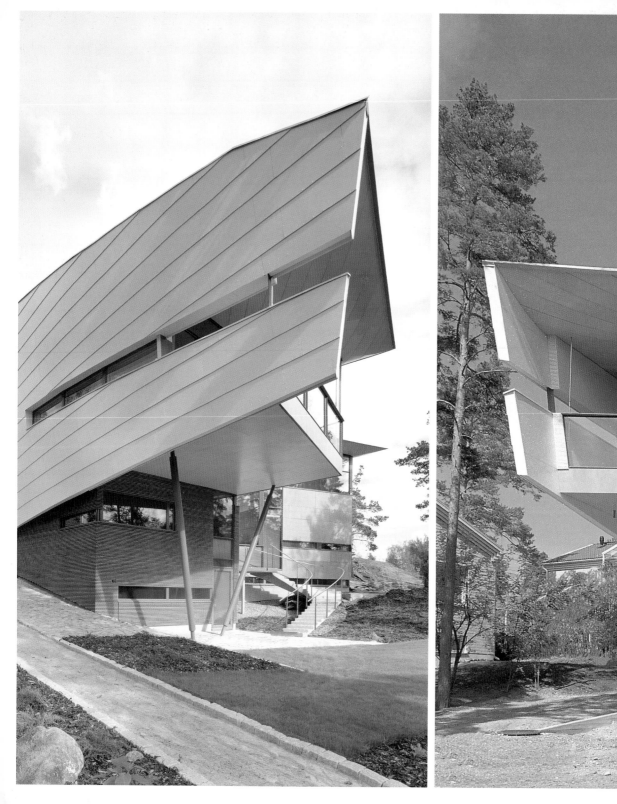

122-123: Plants blooming in weathered wooden chests are a small-scale reflection of the spectacular natural backdrop.

122-123 : Les plantes fleuries des pots en bois, teints pour les protéger des intempéries, répondent à échelle réduite à l'imposant décor naturel.

122-123: Blühende Pflanzen in hölzernen, von der Witterung verfärbten Pflanzkästen nehmen in kleinerem Maßstab die eindrucksvolle Naturkulisse der Landschaft auf.

126-129: Each of the four town houses possesses a generous balcony that extends over two storeys. Viewed as a whole, one sees a cool, ultra-modern loggia in a harbour setting.

126-129 : Les quatre maisons de ville disposent chacune d'un vaste balcon qui s'étend sur deux étages. Les piliers et la pergola créent une sorte de loggia.

126-129: Jedes der vier Town Houses verfügt über einen großzügigen Balkon, der sich über zwei Geschosse erstreckt. Die Stützen und eine Pergola lassen eine Art Loggia entstehen.

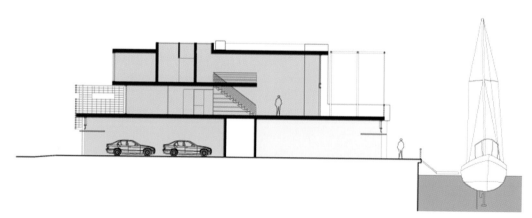

Section Section Schnitt

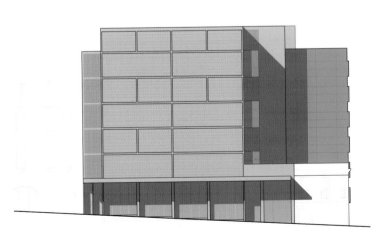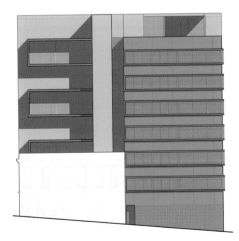

Elevation Élévation Aufriss

-135: The façade of this apartment block is nothing but balcony! The roof accommodates two luxurious penthouses, where the artistry evident in the façade has been
ated in two large terraces.

-135 : La façade de cet immeuble donne l'impression de n'être qu'un seul balcon. Sur le toit, deux luxurieux attiques transforment chacun l'élément créatif de la
de en une terrasse spacieuse.

-135: Die Fassade dieses Apartmentblocks wirkt wie ein einziger Balkon. Auf dem Dach befinden sich zwei luxuriöse Penthouses, die das gestalterische Element der
sade jeweils in eine großzügige Terrasse umsetzen.

Subpenthouse Plan Plan sous attique Subpenthouse-Grundriss

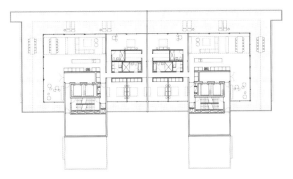

Penthouse Plan Plan de l'appartement Penthouse-Grundriss

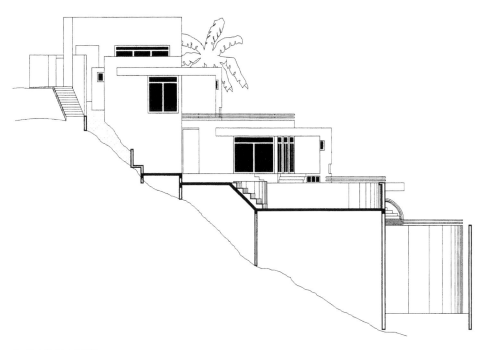

Section Section Schnitt

-145: Through the use of coloured, transparent plastic panels in the balustrade, each apartment takes on an individual character. The view outside is transformed ugh the colour, which lets familiar things appear in a new light.

-145 : L'utilisation de panneaux en plastique transparent teinté en guise de balustrade confère un caractère personnel à chaque appartement. La couleur dénature erception visuelle, faisant apparaître ce qui est familier de l'autre côté sous un jour nouveau.

-145: Durch die Verwendung eingefärbter, transparenter Kunststoffplatten als Balkonbrüstung erhält jede Wohnung einen individuellen Charakter. Der Blick nach ußen wird durch die Farbe verfremdet und lässt Bekanntes in neuem Licht erscheinen.

5-149: The plant pattern imprinted on the transparent balustrade appears to be a poetic, perhaps also ironic, commentary on the stony city.

5-149 : Le motif végétal imprimé sur les balustrades transparentes semble se transformer en commentaire poétique, voire ironique, sur la ville de pierre.

5-149: Das auf die transparenten Balkonbrüstungen aufgedruckte Pflanzenmuster wirkt wie ein poetischer, vielleicht auch ironischer Kommentar auf die steinerne Stadt.

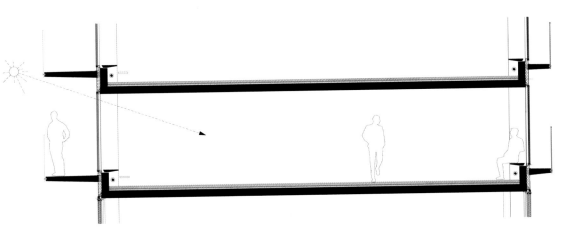

Details Détails Details

150-151: What often ends up as a superfluous, triangular expanse of building material has become in this case a dramatically-shaped balcony that suggests a ship's prow

150-151 : L'extrémité triangulaire, genre de surface trop souvent négligée ailleurs, a été ici transformée en un surprenant balcon pouvant évoquer la proue d'un navire.

150-151: Was oft genug als dreieckige Restfläche endet, ist in diesem Fall ein dramatisch geformter Balkon geworden, der einen Schiffsbug assoziieren lässt.

152-154: In this project, too, the ship metaphor is unmistakeable: the dynamic lines, the use of white, the railing and the triangular balcony in front like a powerful prow evoke a luxury yacht.

152-154 : Là aussi, la métaphore maritime saute aux yeux : les lignes dynamiques, le choix du blanc, le bastingage à barres horizontales et le triangle du balcon s'avançant telle la proue d'un immense navire font penser à un yacht luxueux.

152-154: Auch bei diesem Projekt ist die Schiffsmetaphorik unübersehbar: Die dynamischen Linien, die Verwendung der Farbe Weiß, die horizontal gegliederte Reling und das wie ein mächtiger Bug vorn auslaufende Dreieck des Balkons erinnern an eine Luxusyacht.

155-157: Positioned directly above the surf, the balcony still exudes cosiness through the use of soft cushions and pastel tones.

155-157 : Situé juste au-dessus des vagues qui déferlent, ce balcon dégage néanmoins une atmosphère très agréable grâce aux coussins moelleux et aux tons pastel des matelas et coussins.

155-157: Unmittelbar über der Brandung des Meeres gelegen, strahlt der Balkon durch die Verwendung von weichen Polstern und Pastelltönen dennoch eine große Behaglichkeit aus.

160–161: This terrace is the perfect extension of the living room into the coastal landscape. The encircling beam transforms the terrace into a part of the house that is open on all sides.

160–161 : La terrasse est le prolongement parfait du salon dans le paysage côtier. La poutre qui en fait le tour la transforme en espace de la maison, ouvert de tous côtés.

160–161: Diese Terrasse ist eine perfekte Fortsetzung des Wohnraums in die Küstenlandschaft hinein. Der umlaufende Balken macht die Terrasse zu einem Teil des Hauses, der nach allen Seiten hin offen ist.

-164: This roof terrace — with its totally original shape, varied materials that harmonise wonderfully and, last but not least, shatter-proof glass balustrade — tterly spectacular!

-164 : Le toit de cette terrasse est tout simplement spectaculaire, de par sa forme unique en son genre, l'association parfaite des différents matériaux et alustrade en verre incassable !

-164: Diese Dachterrasse ist durch ihre einzigartige Form, die wunderbar aufeinander abgestimmten verschiedenen Materialien und nicht zuletzt die mit bruchsicherem s gefertigte Brüstung schlichtweg spektakulär!

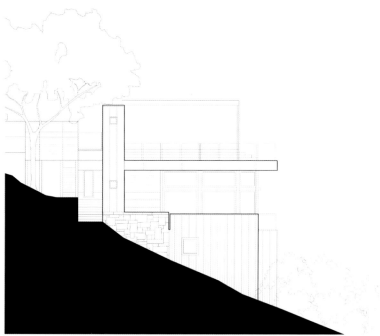

Elevation Élévation Aufriss

-167: The transition from this completely glass-enclosed living room to the outdoors is so subtle and smooth that the living room almost seems like a part of the roof ace instead of the other way round.

-167 : Le passage du salon entièrement vitré à l'extérieur est si subtil et discret que l'intérieur semble presque faire partie de la terrasse, au lieu du contraire.

-167: Der Übergang von diesem komplett verglasten Wohnraum nach außen ist so subtil und fließend, dass der Wohnraum beinahe wie ein Teil der Dachterrasse t, und nicht umgekehrt.

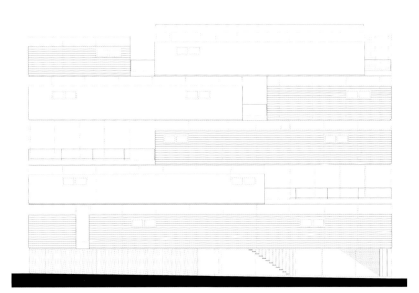

Elevation Élévation Aufriss

-169: Undulating, brown-coloured pre-fabricated concrete bands, whose rough surface is reminiscent of wood grain, wrap around the building. The top-floor loggias protected from the wind.

-169 : Des éléments préfabriqués en béton brun aux formes irrégulières, dont la structure grossière rappelle les veines du bois, entourent le bâtiment. À l'étage érieur se trouvent des loggias protégées du vent.

-169: Unregelmäßig geformte und braun eingefärbte Betonfertigteile, deren grobe Struktur an eine Holzmaserung denken lässt, umhüllen die Gebäudevolumen. ler obersten Etage befinden sich windgeschützte Loggien.

Elevation Élévation Aufriss

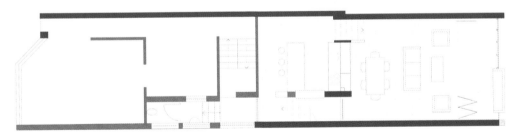

Plan Plan Grundriss

2-175: The wooden slats, combined with the ceiling and canopy, break up the incoming light and create ever-shifting patterns of light and shadow. In this way, cessive amounts of sunshine are avoided.

2-175 : La lumière qui pénètre à travers les lattes de bois et le plafond est déviée plusieurs fois, créant un vif jeu d'ombre et de lumière. Le balcon prévient cependant ut ensoleillement excessif.

2-175: Das durch die Holzlatten und die Decke einfallende Licht wird vielfach gebrochen, wodurch ein lebhaftes Schattenspiel entsteht. Eine übermäßige nneneinstrahlung wird dennoch verhindert.

178-181: The extraordinary shape of this residential tower enabled the balconies to be installed on alternating sides of the building, creating large open spaces that are protected from the sun.

178-181 : La forme particulière de la tour d'habitation a permis de placer les balcons alternativement de différents côtés, de manière à créer des espaces ouverts hauts et vastes mais protégés du soleil.

178-181: Die besondere Form des Wohnturms ermöglichte es, die Balkone abwechselnd an verschiedenen Seiten des Gebäudes anzubringen, sodass hohe, großzügige, aber dennoch sonnengeschützte Freibereiche geschaffen werden konnten.

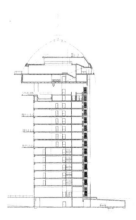

Section Section Schnitt

Plan Plan Grundriss

Side elevation Élévation latérale Seitenansicht

2-185: This building — named "Spaceship" by the architect — features terraced balconies, stacked on top of each other. Due to occasional flooding in this desert area, house is built on stilts. The design of the steel balustrades "quotes" the architecture of Frank Lloyd Wright.

2-185 : Les balcons du bâtiment baptisé « Vaisseau spatial » par l'architecte forment des terrasses superposées. En raison des inondations se produisant parfois ns cette région désertique, la maison est construite sur pilotis. La forme des balustrades en acier décline l'architecture de Frank Lloyd Wright.

2-185: Die Balkone des vom Architekten „Spaceship" genannten Gebäudes sind terrassenförmig übereinander angeordnet. Wegen gelegentlich auftretender erschwemmungen in dieser Wüstenlandschaft ist das Haus aufgeständert. Die Formgebung der stählernen Brüstungen zitiert die Architektur von Frank Lloyd Wright.

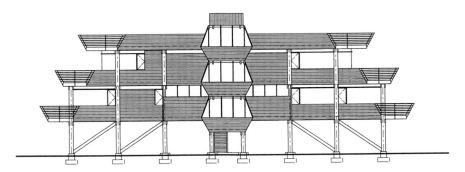

Front elevation Elévation frontale Vorderansicht

187: A balcony that reminds you of a race track. The large projecting roof guards against the midday sun.

187 : La forme de ce balcon évoque un hippodrome ou une piste de course. Le grand avant-toit protège du soleil de midi.

187: Ein Balkon, dessen Formgebung an eine Rennbahn erinnert. Das weite Vordach schützt vor der hoch stehenden Sonne.

Photo Credits • Crédits photographiques • Fotonachweis

Adam Butler
54-55

Agi Simoes/Zapaimages
170-171

**Alberto Burckhardt,
Beatriz Santo Domingo**
78-79

Alejo Bagué
44-47

Barclay & Carousse
14-17

Ben Wrigley
28-29

Bill Timmerman
6, 118-119

Chris Ott
40-41

Christian Richters
168-169

Dao Lou Zha
18-21

David Hecht/Tannerhecht
126-129

David Joseph
22-25

Duccio Malagamba
60-61, 66-67

Eduardo Consuegra
74-77

Eric Sierens
172-175, 189

Fernando Alda
188

Ger van der Vlugt
106-107

Gianni Basso/Vega MG
5, 80-81

Giulio Oriani/Vega MG
42-43

Gogortza/Llorella
2

Herman van Doorn
124-125

Joan Roig
30-33, 158-161

John Ellis
84-85

John Wheatley
26-27

Jordi Miralles
34-37, 62-65, 68-71,
152-154

José Luis Hausmann
99-103

Jyrki Tasa
116-117, 120-121

Lew Rodin
142-145

Luuk Kramer
108-111

Manos Meisen
10

Matteo Piazza
72-73, 138-141

Miquel Tres
5, 155-157

Nelson Kon
48-51, 52-53, 86-89

Nils Petter Dale
112-115

Oscar Necoechea
165-167

Patrick Wong
162-164

Paul Ott
82-83, 136-137

Philippe Ruault
96-98

R. Borden, L. Wilson, C. Mead
182-185

Roger Casas
192

Ross Honeysett
130-131, 132-135

Rupert Steiner
146-149

Shania Shegedyn
56-59, 90-91, 92-95

Undine Pröhl
8, 38-39, 122-123, 150-151,
176-177, 186-187

Yael Pincus
178-181